And God Spoke

A Message God Spoke to Me.
A Study of His Heart and Will for Your Life.

VOLUME II

DIANE ROSSI

WestBow Press books may be ordered through booksellers or by contacting:

WestBow Press
A Division of Thomas Nelson & Zondervan
1663 Liberty Drive
Bloomington, IN 47403
www.westbowpress.com
844-714-3454

ISBN: 978-1-6642-5759-7 (sc)
ISBN: 978-1-6642-5758-0 (e)

Library of Congress Control Number: 2022902725

Print information available on the last page.

WestBow Press rev. date: 12/05/2022

“In the beginning was
the Word, and the Word
was with God, and
the Word was God.”

–John 1:1

Preface

Whereas the theme of volume I of *And God Spoke* was about repentance, the theme of Volume II is about preparing our hearts to usher in a mighty move of the Holy Spirit. Get ready to watch what God can do when we give Him the freedom to move.

The message for this book was received one day while praying. I just kept writing page after page of what I was hearing. When I went back to reread what I had written, I realized that the statements were based on scriptures. I felt prompted urgently to share this message with others so that they may experience complete freedom in God.

While I was receiving the message, I had several what I would call mini visions. In one of them, I saw the roofs of numerous churches. Rising from their rooftops were boxes that were illuminated as they were opened. The illumination represented complete freedom and the release of the Holy Spirit. *It is time to open the boxes.*

Before you read any further, please pray and ask God to open your mind and heart to what He wants to speak to you through this book.

Open the Boxes—Setting God Free to Move

I feel like a child waiting for Christmas morning. I've just heard the word *flood*. Once those waters start to flow, there will be no dam that can hold them back. This is what God has been wanting to give His people—Himself and all of Himself. We have to want it. We have to press in.

We have to learn to praise God at all times. Praising when you don't want to. Praising when your answer has not come. Praising when you feel like the storm is going to take you out. Praising when you want to quit. Praising when all others tell you it won't work. Praising until the heavens open up and begin to rain. Praising until the flood of God sweeps His people away.

God is stirring up something big. I mean big. We are going to see the captives set free. Breakthroughs. The release of the Holy Spirit like a rushing wind. Fire raining down. Healings. Deliverance. Wind. Rain. Fire. Victory. There will be dancing. There will be shouting. There will be weeping but only for a moment. The chains will be broken. The heaviness will be lifted. Freedom will replace bondage. Curses will be broken. Words of encouragement will replace the negative ones that have been spoken. When the Spirit is free to move, mighty things will happen. Heaven will come down. God will meet His people. Get ready to celebrate what He is going to do.

Learning God's Heart and Will for Your Life

How often have you contained God by your beliefs, indoctrinations, or others' interpretations of His Word? God requests that you be completely and unabashedly open to Him and what He desires. He does not want you to limit Him by your preconceived ideas of who He is or what He can accomplish. Rather, He wants you to search His Word in its entirety while praying for understanding to learn His true character and how to be positioned in His will.

Do you want to experience a new level of intimacy with God? Then wholeheartedly put aside your own desires and agendas, aligning yourself to be in a complete relationship Him. You were created to be in communion with God, to offer Him praises, and to share His love with others. That is His will.

How to Use This Study

It is recommended that you have a Bible, a good concordance or internet connection for searching for scriptures, an additional notebook, and a pad of large sticky notes or index cards while you do this study.

This is a self-guided study with the intention of *you* learning what God wants to teach *you* from His Word. As you progress through the study, you may come across words or phrases that are similar to ones you have already explored. Use this as an opportunity to dig even deeper into what God wants you to learn. This is not a study to rush through. In fact, each message should be thoroughly analyzed before moving on to the next one.

Before each study, earnestly pray and ask God for guidance, revelation, insight, and clarity of mind. Pray that He will reveal to you what He wants you to learn from the message. Remove environmental and mental distractions. You will want uninterrupted, unencumbered time with God to be able to hear what He will say to you. Ask God to remove any hindrances in your life that would keep you from hearing His voice and truth.

Open the book to the message you are working on. Read it. Then make it into a prayer that is personal to you. For example, the prayer for the first message could be, "Father God, today I am asking You to give me what I need to fulfill Your purposes with my life."

Write this message on a sticky note or index card. You may want more than one. Put it on your car dash, your bathroom mirror, your refrigerator, or anywhere you are likely to see it during the day. Each time you see it, pray the personal prayer and ask God to show you how to apply this to your life.

On the pages after the message, fill out the responses to each of the questions or statements. If you find the space limiting, use a notebook for additional space.

Opening Prayer

Dear God,

Today I ask that You open my spiritual eyes. I ask that as I press into You and read Your Word, You will reveal Yourself to me. I know that at times my spiritual legs are weak. Forgive me for the times that I fail to trust in You and Your promises. Strengthen me in mind and spirit that I may commune with You and feel Your presence.

Make me aware of Your Holy Spirit and His desire to work in my life. Thank You for providing one to intercede on my behalf, to comfort me, and to seal me with the testament that I am Your child. Give to me the gifts that I need to operate according to what *You want me to do.*

Amen.

You have not because you ask not.

—And God spoke

Date:____________________ Theme of message: ____________________________________

My personal prayer for today's message is:

How does this message apply to me?

▷ Search the Bible for scriptures applicable to the message. Write them in your notebook. Be sure to include the scripture reference.

What has God spoken to you through this message?

How can you use this message to show God's unconditional love to others?

▷ Write any notes or additional thoughts in your notebook.

You try to put
Me in a box.

—And God spoke

Date:____________________ Theme of message: ______________________________

My personal prayer for today's message is:

How does this message apply to me?

▷ Search the Bible for scriptures applicable to the message. Write them in your notebook. Be sure to include the scripture reference.

What has God spoken to you through this message?

How can you use this message to show God's unconditional love to others?

▷ Write any notes or additional thoughts in your notebook.

I cannot be contained.

—And God spoke

Date:____________________ Theme of message: ____________________________________

My personal prayer for today's message is:

How does this message apply to me?

▷ Search the Bible for scriptures applicable to the message. Write them in your notebook. Be sure to include the scripture reference.

What has God spoken to you through this message?

How can you use this message to show God's unconditional love to others?

▷ Write any notes or additional thoughts in your notebook.

Give Him glory,
honor, and praise.

—And God spoke

Date:____________________ Theme of message: ______________________________

My personal prayer for today's message is:

____

____

____

____

____

How does this message apply to me?

____

____

____

____

____

▷ Search the Bible for scriptures applicable to the message. Write them in your notebook. Be sure to include the scripture reference.

What has God spoken to you through this message?

____

____

____

____

____

How can you use this message to show God's unconditional love to others?

____

____

____

____

____

____

▷ Write any notes or additional thoughts in your notebook.

I will finish what
I started.

—And God spoke

Date:____________________ Theme of message: ______________________________

My personal prayer for today's message is:

How does this message apply to me?

▷ Search the Bible for scriptures applicable to the message. Write them in your notebook. Be sure to include the scripture reference.

What has God spoken to you through this message?

How can you use this message to show God's unconditional love to others?

▷ Write any notes or additional thoughts in your notebook.

My plans are My plans.

—And God spoke

Date:____________________ Theme of message: ________________________________

My personal prayer for today's message is:

How does this message apply to me?

▷ Search the Bible for scriptures applicable to the message. Write them in your notebook. Be sure to include the scripture reference.

What has God spoken to you through this message?

How can you use this message to show God's unconditional love to others?

▷ Write any notes or additional thoughts in your notebook.

You were not created
for you but for Me
and My pleasure.

—And God spoke

Date:_____________________ Theme of message: ____________________________________

My personal prayer for today's message is:

How does this message apply to me?

▷ Search the Bible for scriptures applicable to the message. Write them in your notebook. Be sure to include the scripture reference.

What has God spoken to you through this message?

How can you use this message to show God's unconditional love to others?

▷ Write any notes or additional thoughts in your notebook.

I want fellowship with you.

—And God spoke

Date:____________________ Theme of message: ______________________________

My personal prayer for today's message is:

____

____

____

____

____

How does this message apply to me?

____

____

____

____

____

▷ Search the Bible for scriptures applicable to the message. Write them in your notebook. Be sure to include the scripture reference.

What has God spoken to you through this message?

____

____

____

____

____

How can you use this message to show God's unconditional love to others?

____

____

____

____

____

____

▷ Write any notes or additional thoughts in your notebook.

You cannot outgive Me.

—And God spoke

Date:____________________ Theme of message: ____________________________________

My personal prayer for today's message is:

____
____
____
____
____

How does this message apply to me?

____
____
____
____
____

▷ Search the Bible for scriptures applicable to the message. Write them in your notebook. Be sure to include the scripture reference.

What has God spoken to you through this message?

____
____
____
____
____

How can you use this message to show God's unconditional love to others?

____
____
____
____
____
____

▷ Write any notes or additional thoughts in your notebook.

You cannot outthink Me.

—And God spoke

Date:____________________ Theme of message: ______________________________

My personal prayer for today's message is:

How does this message apply to me?

▷ Search the Bible for scriptures applicable to the message. Write them in your notebook. Be sure to include the scripture reference.

What has God spoken to you through this message?

How can you use this message to show God's unconditional love to others?

▷ Write any notes or additional thoughts in your notebook.

I knew you before the foundations of the earth.

—And God spoke

Date:____________________ Theme of message: ____________________________________

My personal prayer for today's message is:

How does this message apply to me?

▷ Search the Bible for scriptures applicable to the message. Write them in your notebook. Be sure to include the scripture reference.

What has God spoken to you through this message?

How can you use this message to show God's unconditional love to others?

▷ Write any notes or additional thoughts in your notebook.

I chose you.

—And God spoke

Date:____________________ Theme of message: ________________________________

My personal prayer for today's message is:

____

____

____

____

____

How does this message apply to me?

____

____

____

____

____

▷ Search the Bible for scriptures applicable to the message. Write them in your notebook. Be sure to include the scripture reference.

What has God spoken to you through this message?

____

____

____

____

____

How can you use this message to show God's unconditional love to others?

____

____

____

____

____

____

▷ Write any notes or additional thoughts in your notebook.

I created you with unique talents and gifts to glorify Me.

—And God spoke

Date:____________________ Theme of message: ____________________________________

My personal prayer for today's message is:

How does this message apply to me?

▷ Search the Bible for scriptures applicable to the message. Write them in your notebook. Be sure to include the scripture reference.

What has God spoken to you through this message?

How can you use this message to show God's unconditional love to others?

▷ Write any notes or additional thoughts in your notebook.

Do not limit Me.

—And God spoke

Date:____________________ Theme of message: ______________________________

My personal prayer for today's message is:

How does this message apply to me?

▷ Search the Bible for scriptures applicable to the message. Write them in your notebook. Be sure to include the scripture reference.

What has God spoken to you through this message?

How can you use this message to show God's unconditional love to others?

▷ Write any notes or additional thoughts in your notebook.

I have no boundaries.

—And God spoke

Date:_______________ Theme of message: _______________

My personal prayer for today's message is:

How does this message apply to me?

▷ Search the Bible for scriptures applicable to the message. Write them in your notebook. Be sure to include the scripture reference.

What has God spoken to you through this message?

How can you use this message to show God's unconditional love to others?

▷ Write any notes or additional thoughts in your notebook.

I created boundaries.

—And God spoke

Date:______________________ Theme of message: ______________________________________

My personal prayer for today's message is:

How does this message apply to me?

▷ Search the Bible for scriptures applicable to the message. Write them in your notebook. Be sure to include the scripture reference.

What has God spoken to you through this message?

How can you use this message to show God's unconditional love to others?

▷ Write any notes or additional thoughts in your notebook.

I set the stars in the sky
and the moon in its
place and hung the sun.
What have you done?

—And God spoke

Date:__________________ Theme of message: ____________________________

My personal prayer for today's message is:

How does this message apply to me?

▷ Search the Bible for scriptures applicable to the message. Write them in your notebook. Be sure to include the scripture reference.

What has God spoken to you through this message?

How can you use this message to show God's unconditional love to others?

▷ Write any notes or additional thoughts in your notebook.

Ye of little faith.

—And God spoke

Date:____________________ Theme of message: ____________________________________

My personal prayer for today's message is:

____

____

____

____

____

How does this message apply to me?

____

____

____

____

____

▷ Search the Bible for scriptures applicable to the message. Write them in your notebook. Be sure to include the scripture reference.

What has God spoken to you through this message?

____

____

____

____

____

How can you use this message to show God's unconditional love to others?

____

____

____

____

____

____

▷ Write any notes or additional thoughts in your notebook.

You were planned. You were not a mistake but deliberately planned.

—And God spoke

Date:____________________ Theme of message: ____________________

My personal prayer for today's message is:

____
____
____
____
____

How does this message apply to me?

____
____
____
____
____

▷ Search the Bible for scriptures applicable to the message. Write them in your notebook. Be sure to include the scripture reference.

What has God spoken to you through this message?

____
____
____
____
____

How can you use this message to show God's unconditional love to others?

____
____
____
____
____
____

▷ Write any notes or additional thoughts in your notebook.

Remain faithful
and steadfast.

—And God spoke

Date:____________________ Theme of message: ____________________________________

My personal prayer for today's message is:

How does this message apply to me?

▷ Search the Bible for scriptures applicable to the message. Write them in your notebook. Be sure to include the scripture reference.

What has God spoken to you through this message?

How can you use this message to show God's unconditional love to others?

▷ Write any notes or additional thoughts in your notebook.

Stay the course.

—And God spoke

Date:____________________ Theme of message: ______________________________

My personal prayer for today's message is:

____
____
____
____
____

How does this message apply to me?

____
____
____
____
____

▷ Search the Bible for scriptures applicable to the message. Write them in your notebook. Be sure to include the scripture reference.

What has God spoken to you through this message?

____
____
____
____
____

How can you use this message to show God's unconditional love to others?

____
____
____
____
____
____

▷ Write any notes or additional thoughts in your notebook.

A ship without a rudder
soon goes off course.

—And God spoke

Date:____________________ Theme of message: ________________________________

My personal prayer for today's message is:

How does this message apply to me?

▷ Search the Bible for scriptures applicable to the message. Write them in your notebook. Be sure to include the scripture reference.

What has God spoken to you through this message?

How can you use this message to show God's unconditional love to others?

▷ Write any notes or additional thoughts in your notebook.

Let Me steer your direction.

—And God spoke

Date:____________________ Theme of message: ______________________________

My personal prayer for today's message is:

How does this message apply to me?

▷ Search the Bible for scriptures applicable to the message. Write them in your notebook. Be sure to include the scripture reference.

What has God spoken to you through this message?

How can you use this message to show God's unconditional love to others?

▷ Write any notes or additional thoughts in your notebook.

You can just rest in Me.

—And God spoke

Date:____________________ Theme of message: ______________________________

My personal prayer for today's message is:

How does this message apply to me?

▷ Search the Bible for scriptures applicable to the message. Write them in your notebook. Be sure to include the scripture reference.

What has God spoken to you through this message?

How can you use this message to show God's unconditional love to others?

▷ Write any notes or additional thoughts in your notebook.

I have already planned everything.

—And God spoke

Date:____________________ Theme of message: ________________________________

My personal prayer for today's message is:

How does this message apply to me?

▷ Search the Bible for scriptures applicable to the message. Write them in your notebook. Be sure to include the scripture reference.

What has God spoken to you through this message?

How can you use this message to show God's unconditional love to others?

▷ Write any notes or additional thoughts in your notebook.

You will be surprised at how easy it seems when you trust in Me.

—**And God spoke**

Date:____________________ Theme of message: ____________________________________

My personal prayer for today's message is:

____

____

____

____

____

How does this message apply to me?

____

____

____

____

____

▷ Search the Bible for scriptures applicable to the message. Write them in your notebook. Be sure to include the scripture reference.

What has God spoken to you through this message?

____

____

____

____

____

How can you use this message to show God's unconditional love to others?

____

____

____

____

____

____

▷ Write any notes or additional thoughts in your notebook.

My love never fails.

—And God spoke

Date:____________________ Theme of message: ________________________________

My personal prayer for today's message is:

How does this message apply to me?

▷ Search the Bible for scriptures applicable to the message. Write them in your notebook. Be sure to include the scripture reference.

What has God spoken to you through this message?

How can you use this message to show God's unconditional love to others?

▷ Write any notes or additional thoughts in your notebook.

My love is everlasting.

—And God spoke

Date:____________________ Theme of message: ____________________________________

My personal prayer for today's message is:

____

____

____

____

____

How does this message apply to me?

____

____

____

____

____

▷ Search the Bible for scriptures applicable to the message. Write them in your notebook. Be sure to include the scripture reference.

What has God spoken to you through this message?

____

____

____

____

____

How can you use this message to show God's unconditional love to others?

____

____

____

____

____

____

▷ Write any notes or additional thoughts in your notebook.

My love knows no boundaries.

—And God spoke

Date:_________________ Theme of message: _________________________

My personal prayer for today's message is:

____

____

____

____

____

How does this message apply to me?

____

____

____

____

____

▷ Search the Bible for scriptures applicable to the message. Write them in your notebook. Be sure to include the scripture reference.

What has God spoken to you through this message?

____

____

____

____

____

How can you use this message to show God's unconditional love to others?

____

____

____

____

____

____

▷ Write any notes or additional thoughts in your notebook.

Petition for more of Me.

—And God spoke

Date:____________________ Theme of message: ________________________________

My personal prayer for today's message is:

How does this message apply to me?

▷ Search the Bible for scriptures applicable to the message. Write them in your notebook. Be sure to include the scripture reference.

What has God spoken to you through this message?

How can you use this message to show God's unconditional love to others?

▷ Write any notes or additional thoughts in your notebook.

I want more of you.

—And God spoke

Date:____________________ Theme of message: ______________________________

My personal prayer for today's message is:

____

____

____

____

____

How does this message apply to me?

____

____

____

____

____

▷ Search the Bible for scriptures applicable to the message. Write them in your notebook. Be sure to include the scripture reference.

What has God spoken to you through this message?

____

____

____

____

____

How can you use this message to show God's unconditional love to others?

____

____

____

____

____

____

▷ Write any notes or additional thoughts in your notebook.

Obedience is a must.

—And God spoke

Date:____________________ Theme of message: ______________________________

My personal prayer for today's message is:

How does this message apply to me?

▷ Search the Bible for scriptures applicable to the message. Write them in your notebook. Be sure to include the scripture reference.

What has God spoken to you through this message?

How can you use this message to show God's unconditional love to others?

▷ Write any notes or additional thoughts in your notebook.

Take up your cross and follow Me—only Me.

-and God spoke

Date:____________________ Theme of message: ____________________

My personal prayer for today's message is:

How does this message apply to me?

▷ Search the Bible for scriptures applicable to the message. Write them in your notebook. Be sure to include the scripture reference.

What has God spoken to you through this message?

How can you use this message to show God's unconditional love to others?

▷ Write any notes or additional thoughts in your notebook.

Be careful of wolves in sheep's clothing.

—And God spoke

Date:____________________ Theme of message: ______________________________

My personal prayer for today's message is:

____

____

____

____

____

How does this message apply to me?

____

____

____

____

____

▷ Search the Bible for scriptures applicable to the message. Write them in your notebook. Be sure to include the scripture reference.

What has God spoken to you through this message?

____

____

____

____

____

How can you use this message to show God's unconditional love to others?

____

____

____

____

____

____

▷ Write any notes or additional thoughts in your notebook.

Lean not on your
own understanding.

—And God spoke

Date:____________________ Theme of message: ____________________

My personal prayer for today's message is:

How does this message apply to me?

▷ Search the Bible for scriptures applicable to the message. Write them in your notebook. Be sure to include the scripture reference.

What has God spoken to you through this message?

How can you use this message to show God's unconditional love to others?

▷ Write any notes or additional thoughts in your notebook.

In all your ways acknowledge Me.

—**And God spoke**

Date:____________________ Theme of message: ____________________

My personal prayer for today's message is:

____
____
____
____
____

How does this message apply to me?

____
____
____
____
____

▷ Search the Bible for scriptures applicable to the message. Write them in your notebook. Be sure to include the scripture reference.

What has God spoken to you through this message?

____
____
____
____
____

How can you use this message to show God's unconditional love to others?

____
____
____
____
____
____

▷ Write any notes or additional thoughts in your notebook.

Do not worry about
what the world thinks.

—And God spoke

Date:____________________ Theme of message: ______________________________

My personal prayer for today's message is:

How does this message apply to me?

▷ Search the Bible for scriptures applicable to the message. Write them in your notebook. Be sure to include the scripture reference.

What has God spoken to you through this message?

How can you use this message to show God's unconditional love to others?

▷ Write any notes or additional thoughts in your notebook.

You are not of this world.

—And God spoke

Date:____________________ Theme of message: ______________________________

My personal prayer for today's message is:

How does this message apply to me?

▷ Search the Bible for scriptures applicable to the message. Write them in your notebook. Be sure to include the scripture reference.

What has God spoken to you through this message?

How can you use this message to show God's unconditional love to others?

▷ Write any notes or additional thoughts in your notebook.

You were created
for a high purpose—
My purpose.

-and God spoke

Date:____________________ Theme of message: ________________________________

My personal prayer for today's message is:

____

____

____

____

____

How does this message apply to me?

____

____

____

____

____

▷ Search the Bible for scriptures applicable to the message. Write them in your notebook. Be sure to include the scripture reference.

What has God spoken to you through this message?

____

____

____

____

____

How can you use this message to show God's unconditional love to others?

____

____

____

____

____

____

▷ Write any notes or additional thoughts in your notebook.

Be My church.

—And God spoke

Date:____________________ Theme of message: ____________________

My personal prayer for today's message is:

How does this message apply to me?

▷ Search the Bible for scriptures applicable to the message. Write them in your notebook. Be sure to include the scripture reference.

What has God spoken to you through this message?

How can you use this message to show God's unconditional love to others?

▷ Write any notes or additional thoughts in your notebook.

Be My hands.

—And God spoke

Date:____________________ Theme of message: ______________________________

My personal prayer for today's message is:

____

____

____

____

____

How does this message apply to me?

____

____

____

____

____

▷ Search the Bible for scriptures applicable to the message. Write them in your notebook. Be sure to include the scripture reference.

What has God spoken to you through this message?

____

____

____

____

____

How can you use this message to show God's unconditional love to others?

____

____

____

____

____

____

▷ Write any notes or additional thoughts in your notebook.

Be My heart.

—And God spoke

Date:____________________ Theme of message: ____________________

My personal prayer for today's message is:

____
____
____
____
____

How does this message apply to me?

____
____
____
____
____

▷ Search the Bible for scriptures applicable to the message. Write them in your notebook. Be sure to include the scripture reference.

What has God spoken to you through this message?

____
____
____
____
____

How can you use this message to show God's unconditional love to others?

____
____
____
____
____
____

▷ Write any notes or additional thoughts in your notebook.

Be faithful in all things.

—And God spoke

Date:____________________ Theme of message: ____________________

My personal prayer for today's message is:

How does this message apply to me?

▷ Search the Bible for scriptures applicable to the message. Write them in your notebook. Be sure to include the scripture reference.

What has God spoken to you through this message?

How can you use this message to show God's unconditional love to others?

▷ Write any notes or additional thoughts in your notebook.

Be obedient in all things.

—And God spoke

Date:____________________ Theme of message: ______________________________

My personal prayer for today's message is:

How does this message apply to me?

▷ Search the Bible for scriptures applicable to the message. Write them in your notebook. Be sure to include the scripture reference.

What has God spoken to you through this message?

How can you use this message to show God's unconditional love to others?

▷ Write any notes or additional thoughts in your notebook.

Put away childish things.
It is time for solid things.

—And God spoke

Date:____________________ Theme of message: ____________________

My personal prayer for today's message is:

How does this message apply to me?

▷ Search the Bible for scriptures applicable to the message. Write them in your notebook. Be sure to include the scripture reference.

What has God spoken to you through this message?

How can you use this message to show God's unconditional love to others?

▷ Write any notes or additional thoughts in your notebook.

Everything has a season.

—And God spoke

Date:____________________ Theme of message: ____________________

My personal prayer for today's message is:

How does this message apply to me?

▷ Search the Bible for scriptures applicable to the message. Write them in your notebook. Be sure to include the scripture reference.

What has God spoken to you through this message?

How can you use this message to show God's unconditional love to others?

▷ Write any notes or additional thoughts in your notebook.

My season has come.

—And God spoke

Date:____________________ Theme of message: ____________________________________

My personal prayer for today's message is:

How does this message apply to me?

▷ Search the Bible for scriptures applicable to the message. Write them in your notebook. Be sure to include the scripture reference.

What has God spoken to you through this message?

How can you use this message to show God's unconditional love to others?

▷ Write any notes or additional thoughts in your notebook.

I have heard the prayers of My people.

—And God spoke

Date:____________________ Theme of message: ______________________________

My personal prayer for today's message is:

How does this message apply to me?

▷ Search the Bible for scriptures applicable to the message. Write them in your notebook. Be sure to include the scripture reference.

What has God spoken to you through this message?

How can you use this message to show God's unconditional love to others?

▷ Write any notes or additional thoughts in your notebook.

I will rain down.

—And God spoke

Date:____________________ Theme of message: ______________________________

My personal prayer for today's message is:

How does this message apply to me?

▷ Search the Bible for scriptures applicable to the message. Write them in your notebook. Be sure to include the scripture reference.

What has God spoken to you through this message?

How can you use this message to show God's unconditional love to others?

▷ Write any notes or additional thoughts in your notebook.

A movement like this has never been seen before.

—And God spoke

Date:____________________ Theme of message: ____________________________________

My personal prayer for today's message is:

____

____

____

____

____

How does this message apply to me?

____

____

____

____

____

▷ Search the Bible for scriptures applicable to the message. Write them in your notebook. Be sure to include the scripture reference.

What has God spoken to you through this message?

____

____

____

____

____

How can you use this message to show God's unconditional love to others?

____

____

____

____

____

____

▷ Write any notes or additional thoughts in your notebook.

The glory will fill the temple.

—And God spoke

Date:____________________ Theme of message: ______________________________

My personal prayer for today's message is:

How does this message apply to me?

▷ Search the Bible for scriptures applicable to the message. Write them in your notebook. Be sure to include the scripture reference.

What has God spoken to you through this message?

How can you use this message to show God's unconditional love to others?

▷ Write any notes or additional thoughts in your notebook.

My Spirit will move.

—And God spoke

Date:____________________ Theme of message: ____________________________________

My personal prayer for today's message is:

____

____

____

____

____

How does this message apply to me?

____

____

____

____

____

▷ Search the Bible for scriptures applicable to the message. Write them in your notebook. Be sure to include the scripture reference.

What has God spoken to you through this message?

____

____

____

____

____

How can you use this message to show God's unconditional love to others?

____

____

____

____

____

____

▷ Write any notes or additional thoughts in your notebook.

The blood of Jesus, My beloved Son, that I had to sacrifice for your sins will set the captive free.

—And God spoke

Date:____________________ Theme of message: ____________________________________

My personal prayer for today's message is:

How does this message apply to me?

▷ Search the Bible for scriptures applicable to the message. Write them in your notebook. Be sure to include the scripture reference.

What has God spoken to you through this message?

How can you use this message to show God's unconditional love to others?

▷ Write any notes or additional thoughts in your notebook.

Speak in power
and in truth.

-and God spoke

Date:____________________ Theme of message: ____________________________________

My personal prayer for today's message is:

____

____

____

____

____

How does this message apply to me?

____

____

____

____

____

▷ Search the Bible for scriptures applicable to the message. Write them in your notebook. Be sure to include the scripture reference.

What has God spoken to you through this message?

____

____

____

____

____

How can you use this message to show God's unconditional love to others?

____

____

____

____

____

____

▷ Write any notes or additional thoughts in your notebook.

Guard your heart and mind.

—And God spoke

Date:____________________ Theme of message: ____________________________________

My personal prayer for today's message is:

How does this message apply to me?

▷ Search the Bible for scriptures applicable to the message. Write them in your notebook. Be sure to include the scripture reference.

What has God spoken to you through this message?

How can you use this message to show God's unconditional love to others?

▷ Write any notes or additional thoughts in your notebook.

Remain steadfast.

-and God spoke

Date:____________________ Theme of message: ______________________________

My personal prayer for today's message is:

How does this message apply to me?

▷ Search the Bible for scriptures applicable to the message. Write them in your notebook. Be sure to include the scripture reference.

What has God spoken to you through this message?

How can you use this message to show God's unconditional love to others?

▷ Write any notes or additional thoughts in your notebook.

You do not have to worry about man's favor.

—And God spoke

Date:____________________ Theme of message: ____________________________________

My personal prayer for today's message is:

____
____
____
____
____

How does this message apply to me?

____
____
____
____
____

▷ Search the Bible for scriptures applicable to the message. Write them in your notebook. Be sure to include the scripture reference.

What has God spoken to you through this message?

____
____
____
____
____

How can you use this message to show God's unconditional love to others?

____
____
____
____
____
____

▷ Write any notes or additional thoughts in your notebook.

You have God's favor.

—And God spoke

Date:____________________ Theme of message: ____________________________________

My personal prayer for today's message is:

How does this message apply to me?

▷ Search the Bible for scriptures applicable to the message. Write them in your notebook. Be sure to include the scripture reference.

What has God spoken to you through this message?

How can you use this message to show God's unconditional love to others?

▷ Write any notes or additional thoughts in your notebook.

The time is now.

—And God spoke

Date:____________________ Theme of message: ________________________________

My personal prayer for today's message is:

How does this message apply to me?

▷ Search the Bible for scriptures applicable to the message. Write them in your notebook. Be sure to include the scripture reference.

What has God spoken to you through this message?

How can you use this message to show God's unconditional love to others?

▷ Write any notes or additional thoughts in your notebook.

I have been preparing
My people for now,
to unleash My Spirit,
which has been
anxious to move.

—And God spoke

Date:____________________ Theme of message: ____________________________________

My personal prayer for today's message is:

How does this message apply to me?

▷ Search the Bible for scriptures applicable to the message. Write them in your notebook. Be sure to include the scripture reference.

What has God spoken to you through this message?

How can you use this message to show God's unconditional love to others?

▷ Write any notes or additional thoughts in your notebook.

This will be a movement,
not just a ministry.

—And God spoke

Date:____________________ Theme of message: ________________________________

My personal prayer for today's message is:

____
____
____
____
____

How does this message apply to me?

____
____
____
____
____

▷ Search the Bible for scriptures applicable to the message. Write them in your notebook. Be sure to include the scripture reference.

What has God spoken to you through this message?

____
____
____
____
____

How can you use this message to show God's unconditional love to others?

____
____
____
____
____
____

▷ Write any notes or additional thoughts in your notebook.

Many will be called, but only a few will serve.

—And God spoke

Date:____________________ Theme of message: ________________________________

My personal prayer for today's message is:

How does this message apply to me?

▷ Search the Bible for scriptures applicable to the message. Write them in your notebook. Be sure to include the scripture reference.

What has God spoken to you through this message?

How can you use this message to show God's unconditional love to others?

▷ Write any notes or additional thoughts in your notebook.

I have anointed the ones
I need for this calling.

—And God spoke

Date:____________________ Theme of message: ______________________________

My personal prayer for today's message is:

How does this message apply to me?

▷ Search the Bible for scriptures applicable to the message. Write them in your notebook. Be sure to include the scripture reference.

What has God spoken to you through this message?

How can you use this message to show God's unconditional love to others?

▷ Write any notes or additional thoughts in your notebook.

I am the Alpha and Omega, the Beginning, and the End.

—And God spoke

Date:____________________ Theme of message: ________________________________

My personal prayer for today's message is:

How does this message apply to me?

▷ Search the Bible for scriptures applicable to the message. Write them in your notebook. Be sure to include the scripture reference.

What has God spoken to you through this message?

How can you use this message to show God's unconditional love to others?

▷ Write any notes or additional thoughts in your notebook.

I can start what I want and end what I want. I am in control always.

—And God spoke

Date:____________________ Theme of message: ______________________________

My personal prayer for today's message is:

How does this message apply to me?

▷ Search the Bible for scriptures applicable to the message. Write them in your notebook. Be sure to include the scripture reference.

What has God spoken to you through this message?

How can you use this message to show God's unconditional love to others?

▷ Write any notes or additional thoughts in your notebook.

Do not let gossip
and slander pass
through your lips.

—And God spoke

Date:___________________ Theme of message: ________________________________

My personal prayer for today's message is:

How does this message apply to me?

▷ Search the Bible for scriptures applicable to the message. Write them in your notebook. Be sure to include the scripture reference.

What has God spoken to you through this message?

How can you use this message to show God's unconditional love to others?

▷ Write any notes or additional thoughts in your notebook.

Your purpose is to
speak life, not death.

—**And God spoke**

Date:____________________ Theme of message: ______________________________

My personal prayer for today's message is:

____

____

____

____

____

How does this message apply to me?

____

____

____

____

____

▷ Search the Bible for scriptures applicable to the message. Write them in your notebook. Be sure to include the scripture reference.

What has God spoken to you through this message?

____

____

____

____

____

How can you use this message to show God's unconditional love to others?

____

____

____

____

____

____

▷ Write any notes or additional thoughts in your notebook.

Clean the wound before you heal the wound.

—And God spoke

Date:____________________ Theme of message: ________________________________

My personal prayer for today's message is:

How does this message apply to me?

▷ Search the Bible for scriptures applicable to the message. Write them in your notebook. Be sure to include the scripture reference.

What has God spoken to you through this message?

How can you use this message to show God's unconditional love to others?

▷ Write any notes or additional thoughts in your notebook.

Have you suffered more than Me?

—And God spoke

Date:____________________ Theme of message: ______________________________

My personal prayer for today's message is:

____

____

____

____

____

How does this message apply to me?

____

____

____

____

____

▷ Search the Bible for scriptures applicable to the message. Write them in your notebook. Be sure to include the scripture reference.

What has God spoken to you through this message?

____

____

____

____

____

How can you use this message to show God's unconditional love to others?

____

____

____

____

____

____

▷ Write any notes or additional thoughts in your notebook.

I had to birth My Son knowing He would die a tragic death so you could be saved.

—And God spoke

Date:___________________ Theme of message: _________________________________

My personal prayer for today's message is:

How does this message apply to me?

▷ Search the Bible for scriptures applicable to the message. Write them in your notebook. Be sure to include the scripture reference.

What has God spoken to you through this message?

How can you use this message to show God's unconditional love to others?

▷ Write any notes or additional thoughts in your notebook.

I cannot come to the party without an invitation.

—And God spoke

Date:____________________ Theme of message: ____________________________________

My personal prayer for today's message is:

How does this message apply to me?

▷ Search the Bible for scriptures applicable to the message. Write them in your notebook. Be sure to include the scripture reference.

What has God spoken to you through this message?

How can you use this message to show God's unconditional love to others?

▷ Write any notes or additional thoughts in your notebook.

You cannot do more than God, give more than God, know more than God, or create more than God.

—And God spoke

Date:____________________ Theme of message: ______________________________

My personal prayer for today's message is:

How does this message apply to me?

▷ Search the Bible for scriptures applicable to the message. Write them in your notebook. Be sure to include the scripture reference.

What has God spoken to you through this message?

How can you use this message to show God's unconditional love to others?

▷ Write any notes or additional thoughts in your notebook.

Without God's anointing, one is weak.

—**And God spoke**

Date:____________________ Theme of message: ______________________________

My personal prayer for today's message is:

____

____

____

____

____

How does this message apply to me?

____

____

____

____

____

▷ Search the Bible for scriptures applicable to the message. Write them in your notebook. Be sure to include the scripture reference.

What has God spoken to you through this message?

____

____

____

____

____

How can you use this message to show God's unconditional love to others?

____

____

____

____

____

____

▷ Write any notes or additional thoughts in your notebook.

God will not withhold
any good thing from you.

—And God spoke

Date:____________________ Theme of message: __________________________________

My personal prayer for today's message is:

How does this message apply to me?

▷ Search the Bible for scriptures applicable to the message. Write them in your notebook. Be sure to include the scripture reference.

What has God spoken to you through this message?

How can you use this message to show God's unconditional love to others?

▷ Write any notes or additional thoughts in your notebook.

He will provide.

—And God spoke

Date:____________________ Theme of message: ____________________________

My personal prayer for today's message is:

How does this message apply to me?

▷ Search the Bible for scriptures applicable to the message. Write them in your notebook. Be sure to include the scripture reference.

What has God spoken to you through this message?

How can you use this message to show God's unconditional love to others?

▷ Write any notes or additional thoughts in your notebook.

You will not be focusing on earthly things.

—And God spoke

Date:____________________ Theme of message: ______________________________

My personal prayer for today's message is:

How does this message apply to me?

▷ Search the Bible for scriptures applicable to the message. Write them in your notebook. Be sure to include the scripture reference.

What has God spoken to you through this message?

How can you use this message to show God's unconditional love to others?

▷ Write any notes or additional thoughts in your notebook.

You will not worry about where you live, how you eat, or what you wear. He will provide.

—And God spoke

Date:____________________ Theme of message: ______________________________

My personal prayer for today's message is:

How does this message apply to me?

▷ Search the Bible for scriptures applicable to the message. Write them in your notebook. Be sure to include the scripture reference.

What has God spoken to you through this message?

How can you use this message to show God's unconditional love to others?

▷ Write any notes or additional thoughts in your notebook.

Live the life God has appointed you to live.

—**And God spoke**

Date:____________________ Theme of message: ______________________________

My personal prayer for today's message is:

How does this message apply to me?

▷ Search the Bible for scriptures applicable to the message. Write them in your notebook. Be sure to include the scripture reference.

What has God spoken to you through this message?

How can you use this message to show God's unconditional love to others?

▷ Write any notes or additional thoughts in your notebook.

Give to God all
that He asks.

—And God spoke

Date:____________________ Theme of message: ______________________________

My personal prayer for today's message is:

____

____

____

____

____

How does this message apply to me?

____

____

____

____

____

▷ Search the Bible for scriptures applicable to the message. Write them in your notebook. Be sure to include the scripture reference.

What has God spoken to you through this message?

____

____

____

____

____

How can you use this message to show God's unconditional love to others?

____

____

____

____

____

____

▷ Write any notes or additional thoughts in your notebook.

You cannot outgive God.

—And God spoke

Date:____________________ Theme of message: ________________________________

My personal prayer for today's message is:

____

____

____

____

____

How does this message apply to me?

____

____

____

____

____

▷ Search the Bible for scriptures applicable to the message. Write them in your notebook. Be sure to include the scripture reference.

What has God spoken to you through this message?

____

____

____

____

____

How can you use this message to show God's unconditional love to others?

____

____

____

____

____

____

▷ Write any notes or additional thoughts in your notebook.

Give Me your all—
your very being.

—And God spoke

Date:____________________ Theme of message: ______________________________

My personal prayer for today's message is:

How does this message apply to me?

▷ Search the Bible for scriptures applicable to the message. Write them in your notebook. Be sure to include the scripture reference.

What has God spoken to you through this message?

How can you use this message to show God's unconditional love to others?

▷ Write any notes or additional thoughts in your notebook.

Give Me your mind,
your spirit, your body,
your emotions.

—And God spoke

Date:____________________ Theme of message: ____________________

My personal prayer for today's message is:

____

____

____

____

____

How does this message apply to me?

____

____

____

____

____

▷ Search the Bible for scriptures applicable to the message. Write them in your notebook. Be sure to include the scripture reference.

What has God spoken to you through this message?

____

____

____

____

____

How can you use this message to show God's unconditional love to others?

____

____

____

____

____

____

▷ Write any notes or additional thoughts in your notebook.

Let Me use you.

—And God spoke

Date:____________________ Theme of message: ____________________________________

My personal prayer for today's message is:

____

____

____

____

____

How does this message apply to me?

____

____

____

____

____

▷ Search the Bible for scriptures applicable to the message. Write them in your notebook. Be sure to include the scripture reference.

What has God spoken to you through this message?

____

____

____

____

____

How can you use this message to show God's unconditional love to others?

____

____

____

____

____

____

▷ Write any notes or additional thoughts in your notebook.

Do not remember the former things. I am doing a new thing.

—And God spoke

Date:____________________ Theme of message: ________________________________

My personal prayer for today's message is:

How does this message apply to me?

▷ Search the Bible for scriptures applicable to the message. Write them in your notebook. Be sure to include the scripture reference.

What has God spoken to you through this message?

How can you use this message to show God's unconditional love to others?

▷ Write any notes or additional thoughts in your notebook.

I will make streams in the desert.

—And God spoke

Date:____________________ Theme of message: ______________________________

My personal prayer for today's message is:

____

____

____

____

____

How does this message apply to me?

____

____

____

____

____

▷ Search the Bible for scriptures applicable to the message. Write them in your notebook. Be sure to include the scripture reference.

What has God spoken to you through this message?

____

____

____

____

____

How can you use this message to show God's unconditional love to others?

____

____

____

____

____

____

▷ Write any notes or additional thoughts in your notebook.

I am. Nor was or
will be. I am.

—And God spoke

Epilogue

Do not limit God.

"O Sovereign LORD! You have made the heavens and earth by Your great power. Nothing is too hard for You!" (Jeremiah 32:17).

"You give me strength to attack my enemies and power to overcome their defenses. As for God, His way is perfect: The LORD's word is flawless; He shields all who take refuge in Him" (Psalm 18:29–30).

He can create anything from nothing.

He can speak, and things happen.

He has power over life and death.

He is the beginning and the end.

He cannot contradict His Word.

He is everywhere at all times.

He controls the seasons, time, and nature.

He raises and removes rulers.

He is almighty, all-knowing, and all-powerful.

He has capabilities we cannot comprehend.

He sees everything, knowing even the number of hairs on our heads.

He knows no difficulties.

He is holy.

He is absolute truth.

He provides freedom.

He is righteous.

He is consistent.

His love is never ending.

He is merciful.

He is faithful.

He knew us before we were born.

He is love.

He loves unconditionally.

"Now to the one who can do infinitely more than all we can ask or imagine according to the power that is working among us" (Ephesians 3:20).

"And God is able to make all grace abound to you, so that in all things, at all times, having all that you need, you will abound in every good work" (2 Corinthians 9:8).

God, let us never forget the depth of Your love for us. Help us to see each of Your characteristics at work in our lives. Let us acknowledge You in all things. Teach us how to model You to those who cross our paths. Give us the strength and perseverance to be overcomers of this world. Amen.